EXTREME SURVIVAL

SURVIVING EXTREME SPORTS

Lori Hile

Chicago, Illinois

www.heinemannraintree.com
Visit our website to find out
more information about
Heinemann-Raintree books.

To order:
☎ Phone 888-454-2279
💻 Visit www.heinemannraintree.com
to browse our catalog and order online.

© 2011 Raintree
an imprint of Capstone Global Library, LLC
Chicago, Illinois

Visit our website at
www.heinemannraintree.com

Edited by Adam Miller, Adrian Vigliano, and Andrew
Farrow
Designed by Steve Mead
Original illustrations © Capstone Global Library Ltd.
Illustrated by KJA-Artists.com
Picture research by Tracy Cummins
Production by Camilla Crask
Originated by Capstone Global Library Ltd
Printed and bound in the United States of America,
North Mankato, MN

15 14 13 12 11
10 9 8 7 6 5 4 3 2 1

Library of Congress Cataloging-in-Publication Data
Hile, Lori.
  Surviving extreme sports / Lori Hile.
    p. cm. — (Extreme survival)
  Includes bibliographical references and index.
  ISBN 978-1-4109-3968-5 (hc)
  ISBN 978-1-4109-3975-3 (pb)
1. Extreme sports. 2. Survival skills. I. Title.
  GV749.7.H56 2011
  796.04´6—dc22
2010028689

Acknowledgments
The author and publishers are grateful to the
following for permission to reproduce copyright
material: Alamy p. 40 (© Michael Clark); AP Photo
pp. 43 (Alan Welner), 18 (Reed Saxon); Corbis pp.
34 (©Aaron Poole/NewSport), 47 (©Ben Burgeson/
NewSport), 24 (©Duomo), 35 (©JERRY LAMPEN/
Reuters), 23 (©Joe McBride), 13 (©Les Walker/
NewSport), 14 (©Michael Janosz/isiphotos.com),
7 (©Paul Souders), 15 (©Stephen Frink), 17 (©Ty
Milford/Aurora Photos); Fame Pictures pp. 41 & 46
(Barcroft); Getty Images pp. 20, 8 (Epoque/Pictorial
Parade), 6 (Heinz Kluetmeier/Sports Illustrated), 25
(HENNING KAISER/AFP), 39 (Jamie McGuinness/
Project-Himalaya.com), 11 (Jason Childs), 29
(KAZUHIRO NOGI/AFP), 30 & 31 (Robert Beck/
Sports Illustrated), 32 (Steve Granitz/Wire Image);
Courtesy Jon Comer p. 21; ©Nick Kaloterakis p.
48; Shutterstock pp. 45 (©Christophe Michot), 5
(©Hazan), 37 (©Kraska), 36 (©Mikhail Pogosov),
33 (©szarzynski); Summit Daily News p. 27 (Kristin
Anderson).

Cover photograph of rock climbing reproduced with
the permission of CORBIS/©Tom Stewart.

We would like to thank Ann Fullick for her invaluable
help in the preparation of this book.

CONTENTS

Some words are printed in bold, **like this**. You can find out what they mean by looking in the glossary.

ARE YOU NUTS?!

"Are you nuts?!" Extreme athletes get asked this question a lot. That is because they are constantly challenging themselves to do things that few people have ever seen or imagined to be possible.

In this book, you will read about athletes who dive deep into the ocean without **oxygen**, surf 24-meter (80-foot) walls of water, plunge into a canyon on a skateboard, and scale vertical rock walls without a rope. These athletes have shattered world records—and they have also shattered bones in the process.

Extreme athletes take extreme risks. But that does not mean they are crazy. Many have spent years planning, preparing for, and practicing their feats. When faced with danger or difficult odds, these athletes have had what it takes to survive.

Extreme sports

Extreme sports are activities with high levels of danger. This makes them exciting to perform and to watch. Extreme sports are usually performed by individuals, rather than teams. Some do not have many rules, which allows athletes to be creative and invent new moves or techniques. But extreme sports also require strong technical knowledge and impressive physical skills. A lot of the sports also demand specialized equipment, like a ramp, parachute, or even an airplane!

Some extreme sports, like skateboarding, snowboarding, and BMX, are well known from the **X Games** extreme sports competition. Others may be less familiar, like **BASE jumping**, **free diving**, or **street luge**. You will learn more about these in this book. The list keeps getting longer, as humans continuously look for new ways to push themselves and amaze one another.

WARNING! EXTREME DANGER!

The sports in this book look pretty thrilling. But remember that the athletes performing them are professionals who have practiced their awesome skills and dangerous feats for years. Some even have experts helping them. It is great to admire these pros and let them inspire you. Just don't try their moves at home—or anywhere else!

A BASE jumper plummets down the side of a cliff in Norway.

IN THE DEEP: EXTREME DIVING, SWIMMING, SURFING, AND KAYAKING

Tanya Streeter in action on a dive. Successful free divers must be strong swimmers, and be able to hold their breath for many minutes on end. They must also be able to remain calm and focused when a huge amount of water is between them and a breath of air.

World-record-holding free diver Tanya Streeter moves confidently as she descends into the water. Her goal, and the goal of free divers worldwide, is to dive to incredible depths below the water's surface...with no oxygen tank.

As Tanya goes deeper underwater, her heart rate begins to slow, from 78 beats a minute to only 15. Her blood drains away from her arms and legs and collects in her most **vital organs**, like her heart and her brain. As she descends, Tanya must dodge jellyfish and sharks. When she hits 160 meters (525 feet) below the surface, she turns around and swims back up. After five and a half minutes, she surfaces for air.

Tanya practices **free diving**. Free divers go down as deep into the ocean as possible, often with weights to pull them down, but without oxygen tanks or any safety equipment.

SURVIVAL SCIENCE

How does Tanya do it?

Tanya's success is due in part to a lot of training and planning:

- **Preparation:** To get in shape, Tanya practices **anaerobic** activities, exercises that do not rely on oxygen. She swims underwater laps at a pool, holds her breath as much as she can, and takes many practice dives.
- **Safety:** On each dive, Tanya brings 14 "safety divers" with her, stationed at key points in the water. Several of her competitors have died on dives because they did not bring large enough rescue teams.
- **Blood oxygen levels:** Most people have blood oxygen levels of about 98 percent. Anything below 70 percent is considered dangerous. Scientists measured Tanya's oxygen levels after a dive. After five and half minutes without oxygen, Tanya's level was under 50 percent. A count that low is considered life-threatening for humans. Maybe Tanya is part mermaid!

Why does she do it?

Tanya grew up on the Cayman Islands, near the Caribbean Sea. Free diving since 1997, she dives because she finds the ocean beautiful. She also loves swimming with the best free divers in the world: whales. Without a mask or oxygen tank, Tanya can get close to whales without scaring them. Tanya enjoys pushing both her body and mind to the limit.

Whales are born free divers. A humpback whale (pictured) can dive at least 213 meters (700 feet) deep and hold its breath for 30 minutes. Sperm whales can dive 3,200 meters (10,500 feet) into the ocean!

Extreme swimming: Lynne Cox

If you don't think swimming can be extreme, then you haven't met U.S. swimmer Lynne Cox. Lynne has swum in water cold enough to kill humans and has broken speed records for both men and women.

Swimming to Antarctica

It is 2002, and Lynne looks like she is about to spend a day at the beach. She sits in a boat wearing only a swimsuit, goggles, and a bathing cap. But her destination is the planet's coldest continent: Antarctica. She hopes to become the first person ever to swim a mile in Antarctica's icy waters.

As Lynne jumps from the boat into the ocean, all she can feel is cold. Two rescue vessels hover nearby as she struggles to paddle. Her arms and legs have already turned bright red

Like many marine mammals, extreme swimmer Lynne Cox has an even layer of fat around her body to help keep her warm in freezing water.

from the wintry waters. The water feels thicker and slushier than anything she has ever swum in before—and it is 0°C (32°F). She gasps for oxygen, but cannot get enough. Her lungs are rejecting the frigid air.

Land in sight!

To retain as much body heat as possible, Lynne swims with her head above the cold water. But this creates drag on her body, as if she is swimming uphill. Finally, she tucks her head into the sea to propel herself forward. It is also easier to breathe when her entire body is straight. When she lifts her head, she hears the crew yelling. Lynne is heading for an iceberg! She changes course just in time, although some of the icy crystals scrape her arms and legs.

Now she can see the shore of Antarctica. On it are people and penguins. Not even penguins are swimming today! Lynne smiles. She knows she can make it. She takes a deep breath and shouts, "I'm swimming to Antarctica!" Twenty-five minutes after setting out, Lynne reaches the shore.

SURVIVAL SCIENCE

Frigid temperatures

Water that is 0°C (32°F) would kill most humans in less than five minutes. The human body strives to keep its temperature at a set point we call "normal." When exposed to frigid water, the body must work extra hard to maintain that core temperature. Most humans cannot do it for long.

So, how does Lynne survive? Scientists tested Lynne's temperature for several days. They discovered that her body actually increases in temperature in cold water, rather than decreasing. When she swims this ability reduces the strain on her body. It is possible Lynne has **conditioned** her body to react this way through years of training.

Extreme surfing

Like extreme divers and swimmers, extreme surfers are constantly challenged by the thrills and chills of the ocean.

Learning the ropes of tow-in surfing

U.S. surf legend Laird Hamilton clutches tightly to a rope, as a Jet Ski pulls him toward a 15-meter (50-foot) wave. Then he releases the rope and rips down the face of the monster wave. Laird is practicing the sport he co-founded: **tow-in surfing**.

Most surfers paddle out to waves using their own power. But really big waves are almost impossible to catch. The bigger the wave, the faster it moves. So, paddling to a giant wave would be like chasing a mountain—with the mountain rushing at you. With tow-in surfing, a Jet Ski can "tow" the surfer right into a giant wave.

SURVIVAL TRAINING

Only a handful of surfers can survive such giant waves. To prepare himself for giant drops and huge wipeouts, Laird works out every day with weights, rides a mountain bike, sprints up and down sand dunes, and runs on the beach dragging a 45-kilogram (100-pound) log. And, of course, he spends hours surfing.

The Jet Ski driver tows the surfer into a wave, then shadows the surfer after the rope is released. The Jet Ski must be ready to rush in and rescue the surfer if anything goes wrong.

After being towed into the wave, the surfer releases the rope, and rips down the monster wave.

Big waves, big dangers

With waves as tall as seven-story buildings, every wipeout is life threatening. A 21-meter (70-foot) wave could rip surfers' limbs from their bodies and toss them like rag dolls into the jagged shoreline. Broken bones and slashed skin are so common that Laird stopped counting his stitches after he reached 1,000. If a surfer falls, the Jet Ski driver must race in and pull the surfer aboard, then zoom away before the next big wave crashes down—usually in about 10 seconds. But sometimes even that is not fast enough.

Turn the page to read about Laird Hamilton's most extreme big-wave adventure.

Aerial surfing brings surfers out of the water, into the air.

AERIAL SURFING

Many surfers now borrow a trick or two from skateboarders and snowboarders—and launch flips that send them out of the surf and up into the air. Some surfers say the future of contest surfing will combine aerial maneuvers like these with more traditional surf moves.

Riding giants

When Laird Hamilton awoke on December 3, 2007, he could hear the waves thundering into the North Shore of Maui, the Hawaiian island where he lives. Laird called his longtime surf partner, Brett Lickle, and the two took a Jet Ski out to Jaws, a steep and massive underwater ridge over three-quarters of a kilometer (a half mile) from the shore. When waves hit the ridge, enormous wave swells are produced, making Jaws one of the hottest big-wave surf spots in the world.

That day, the waves were bigger and faster than either man had ever seen. The pair took turns driving the Jet Ski and surfing one giant wave after another. After lunch, Brett towed Laird into a 24-meter (80-foot) monster wave. Laird ripped down the wave's face but had to "bail" (jump over the back of the wave) as the towering giant closed in on him. Brett swooped in to pick Laird up on the Jet Ski, then rushed to escape before the next giant beat down. But the wave was too fast. It pushed both men off the Jet Ski and into the ocean's underbelly.

Beneath the waves

The wave pinned Laird underwater. He waited for his flotation vest to lift him to the surface, only to be pounded by four more giant waves. When both men finally resurfaced, Brett's face was gray. A metal fin from a spare surfboard had sliced skin from the back of his knee all the way down to his ankle. Blood gushed into the water. "I need a **tourniquet**," Brett said. Laird made him one, ripping off his wet suit and tying the sleeves tightly above his friend's wound. Then Laird hurried off to find the Jet Ski, now floating almost half a kilometer (a quarter mile) away. During the 15-minute swim, Laird worried that his friend might bleed to death—or that his blood might attract hungry tiger sharks, which would prey upon him.

As Laird raced back to pick up Brett, he dialed 911 on the radiophone. By the time they reached the shore, an ambulance was waiting. It took 53 stitches to close Brett's wound. But once Laird knew his friend was safe, he found another surf partner and returned to Jaws to ride a few more giants.

"Big-wave riding is like an inner desire that you have, to challenge the sea or to be in harmony with the sea in its most dynamic moment. At Jaws, you can conquer a wave that's [normally] too big, too fast, and too dangerous to ride."

—Laird Hamilton

Laird Hamilton, the king of big-wave surfing, looks like a tiny toy action figure on the face of this giant wave.

Bethany Hamilton: Surfer girl

On October 31, 2003, 13-year-old Bethany Hamilton was floating in the calm seas of her favorite surf spot in Kauai, Hawaii, when she felt a sharp tug on her left arm. The pressure only lasted a few seconds, but Bethany looked down in time to see the flash of a tiger shark. Then she watched the water around her turn "bright red" and realized it was her own blood. The shark had ripped away Bethany's left arm. Bethany used her right arm to paddle out to her best friend, Alana, and Alana's father, Holt, where she calmly announced, "I've been attacked by a shark."

Holt towed Bethany to the beach, then wrapped his surfboard leash (the cord that connects the surfboard to the ankle of the surfer) securely above Bethany's wound, to help stop the bleeding. As Bethany slipped in and out of consciousness, she wondered if she would ever surf again. She had surfed since she could walk. At 13 she was ranked one of the top-eight amateur female surfers in the world.

By the time Bethany arrived at the hospital, she had lost almost 60 percent of the blood in her body. She was given transfusions to replace the lost blood and two surgeries to cleanse and then cover the wound. But three weeks later, Bethany was back out on her board. Climbing on with only one arm was tricky at first but, Bethany says, "Once I was on my feet, everything was easy." After she got back out on the water, she says she cried "happy tears." She started competing again and placed fifth in the National Surfing Championships.

Surfers use their arms for both paddling and balance. After losing her arm, Bethany Hamilton had to learn new ways to balance on her board.

SURVIVAL SCIENCE

How did Bethany survive?

Most people cannot survive losing more than 50 percent of their blood. So, how did Bethany pull through?

- **The tourniquet:** When Holt tied his surfboard leash around Bethany's arm, he saved her life. The leash acted as a tourniquet, which helped slow blood loss from Bethany's vital organs, like her brain and heart.

- **Calmness:** Doctors credit Bethany's calm reaction with helping her survive. Panic would have increased her heart rate and the flow—and loss—of blood.

- **Fitness:** Bethany's high fitness level helped her to survive. Athletes generally have lower blood pressure and pulse rates than average people. If the heart beats more slowly, it also pumps out blood more slowly. Bethany lost a lot of blood, but it oozed out more slowly than it could have.

"I have faith in my goal to be a champion. What else could I do? Stay in bed?"

—Bethany Hamilton, on returning to surfing after her accident

Sharks rarely strike humans, but tiger sharks like this one are responsible for the majority of deadly attacks. Tiger sharks, which can be up to 5 meters (16 feet) long, often take their victims by surprise.

Extreme kayaking

Kayaking has been around for thousands of years, but only in the past century has the paddle sport gone "extreme." Rush Sturges helped take it there. This U.S. kayaker and filmmaker practices **freestyle** kayaking. This means he performs acrobatic moves like flips, cartwheels, and twists with his long, narrow boat, while hurtling down whitewater rivers or rapids. Rush even invented some tricks, including a front flip over a waterfall! But pros like Rush still face extreme challenges, like he did on a 2010 adventure in South America.

Falling flat

Rush climbed into his kayak and paddled toward Argentina's Bonita Falls. The kayaker hit the "record" button on the tiny, waterproof camcorder clipped to his helmet. Rush was making a kayaking film and wanted footage of his plunge down the 18-meter (60-foot) waterfall. As he bounced toward the entrance, his kayak bumped into the right wall of the falls, then the left. To balance, Rush angled his kayak far to the right.

But as Rush crossed the lip of the waterfall, a rock overhang hit the right edge of his kayak and tossed his boat sideways and flat. This is a kayaker's worst nightmare. If a boat plunges into the water flat on its bottom, the kayaker, strapped to the boat, feels a harsh slam on impact. From a tall drop, it is best to nose a kayak into the water front-first. That way, the impact is more gradual—like a swan dive instead of a belly flop. Rush rocked his weight back and forth in an attempt to shift the nose

of the boat down, but it was too late. He landed flat, sitting upright.

Rush coughed and wheezed as the foam and waves bubbled over him. It took him 30 seconds to catch his breath. Rush could move, but his muscles were twitching. He knew he needed help, but the canyon's vertical walls were too steep to climb. Bruised and weak, he managed to steer the last 275 meters (900 feet) of whitewater. A friend rushed him to a hospital, where Rush was diagnosed with a broken back. Fortunately, he had time to recover while he edited his movie. One of the most exciting scenes in the movie is his own jaw-dropping fall!

LESSONS LEARNED

If Rush had to do it again, he would have tucked his body forward when he landed flat. This would have taken some pressure off the base of his spine, which might have prevented his back injury. Another factor in the accident was the water level in the river, which was too low. When Rush landed, the bottom of the boat quickly struck the river floor.

Extreme kayakers must watch for rocks hidden underneath the water, which could spin them off course when plunging over the edge of a giant waterfall.

HIT THE ROAD: SKATEBOARDING, STREET LUGE, BMX, AND RUNNING

Jake Brown flipped from face-first to feet-first as he fell. It is best to land on your back, to spread out the impact more evenly.

The 2007 Summer X Games started out well for Australian skateboarder Jake Brown. He successfully landed a 720 (see box below)—the first time the double spin had ever been performed on a ramp in competition. But as Jake launched into his next move, he lost control of his skateboard high above the 8.5-meter (28-foot) "Mega Ramp." He flailed in midair, then plunged down over 14 meters (47 feet), slamming into the bottom of the ramp. It was one of the hardest hits in skateboarding history.

ROTATION

Many extreme sports moves are known by numbers, not names—for example, 720s, 900s, and 1,280s. That is because they are often measured by degrees of rotation. To better understand degrees, picture yourself standing on a clock, with your head facing the 12. Now, turn your body to face the 3. You have just completed a quarter turn, or a 90-degree rotation. A 180-degree rotation would mean spinning halfway around the circle, to face the 6. A 360-degree spin is one full rotation (back to the 12). As the numbers get higher, the difficulty of the spins increases.

A 720, like the one Jake Brown attempted, consists of two complete **aerial** rotations.

Jake lay **unconscious** for eight minutes, as medics attended to him. Then, miraculously, he stood up and walked out of the stadium, as amazed fans burst into applause. "I just wanted to stand up and make sure my body was working," Jake said. He suffered a **concussion** (brain injury), broken wrist, cracked vertebra, and bruised liver and lung, all of which kept him off his skateboard for six months. But in 2009, two years after his injury, Jake returned to the X Games. He performed in the same "Big Air" competition. This time, he took home a gold medal.

SURVIVAL SCIENCE

Wipeout

How did Jake manage to avoid worse injuries? He spread out the impact of his landing between his ankle, knee, and hip, so no single area took the full impact. It helped, too, that Jake was not spinning or somersaulting when he fell, as that would have made it impossible for him to control his landing position. And, of course, his helmet prevented a much more serious, or deadly, head injury.

2 Jake loses control of his skateboard at his highest point, about 50 feet from the ramp's bottom. He is facing down, head first. He pedals his feet.

3 Halfway down, Jake flips from a face-first fall to feet-first. It is best to land on your back, which spreads the impact more evenly.

1 Jake starts up the 27-foot tall quarterpipe going 40 mph.

4 Jake slams onto the bottom of the pipe feet-first, but quickly falls onto his back. The power of the impact made his shoes fly off his feet.

5 He lands with his arms below him, which probably resulted in the wrist fracture.

EXTREME PRACTICE
Tony suffered many injuries practicing the 900, including a fractured rib.

Extreme skateboarding: Fly like a Hawk

By 1999 U.S. skateboarding legend Tony Hawk had won more medals and invented more moves than any skateboarder in history. But there was one thing he—and no one else—had ever achieved: an in-competition 900. Tony had spent 10 years trying to land the two-and-a-half rotation aerial spin.

At the 1999 Summer X Games, Tony attempted the 900 in the "Best New Trick" competition. He fell. It was after the official competition time, but the crowd wanted him to keep trying. Tony tried again and again, making slight adjustments to his spins each time. On the 11th attempt, he felt a new sensation coming down from the spin: his wheels hitting the ramp! Tony squatted to keep his balance. As he rose up, his fist shot into the air. He'd done it! Since 1999, only three other skaters have landed this difficult and dangerous move.

Jon Comer's story

After losing a limb, a lot of people would rule out a career in professional sports. Not U.S. skateboarder Jon Comer. At age four, Jon's leg was crushed when a car ran over it. His leg had to be **amputated** (cut off) from the knee down, with a **prosthetic** (fake) leg put in its place. At age 10, Jon started skateboarding and decided to go pro someday. He practiced on a ramp in his yard and soon started winning contests.

At 21, Jon became the first professional skateboarder with a prosthetic limb. In his first pro contest, he lost his balance. A security cord caught his leg—and his prosthesis went flying. The crowd gasped, thinking Jon's leg had just been ripped off! Most people who see Jon skate cannot tell his leg is artificial.

SURVIVAL SCIENCE

Energy

Growing up, Tony Hawk was a skinny kid who could not produce enough power to propel himself up large 6-meter (20-foot) **half-pipe** walls. But he found a way. When Tony starts at the top of the U-shaped half-pipe, **gravity** pulls him downward. Gravity is the force that holds us down on Earth's surface. This downward movement creates **kinetic energy**, or the energy of motion, which pushes him to the other side. But to reach the top again, he needs more energy. So, Tony used a technique called "pumping." He bends his knees at the bottom of the ramp, then straightens them on the way up. This raises Tony's center of gravity, which produces enough force to launch him to the top of the ramp—and beyond!

Since Jon Comer cannot feel his prosthetic foot, he has to look down at it frequently, to make sure it stays in the right position.

Street luge: It's all downhill

U.S. athlete David Dean lies flat on his back on an oversized skateboard about 2.4 meters (8 feet) long. He careens down a sloping road, feet first, at 130 kilometers (80 miles) per hour. His body is only 5 centimeters (2 inches) above the ground. David's head is propped on a slightly elevated headrest, so he can see where he is going. His feet rest on foot pegs at the bottom of the sled. There is no motor—only the force of gravity to pull him downhill. David "steers" right by leaning to the right and left by leaning left. To stop, he uses his feet. David brakes faster than most cars.

SURVIVAL SCIENCE

G-force

What keeps **street lugers** from flying off their boards as they whiz down hills? It is something called g-force. Short for "gravitational force," g-force is a pressure that acts on the body. Our bodies are used to the force of gravity. Earth's gravity is defined as 1 g. When your body speeds up or changes direction, the pressure can be greater than the force of gravity. For example, 2g (twice the force of gravity) makes your body feel twice as heavy as usual. In street luge, g-force acts like a natural seatbelt. As lugers speed up, their bodies are crushed back onto their sled by a force of 2g.

But g-force can also hinder athletes. Skateboarders feel up to 2.5g of force on their first descent to the bottom of a ramp, where the ramp curves from vertical to horizontal. For a 50-kilogram (200-pound) skater, it suddenly feels as though he or she weighs 125 kilograms (500 pounds), which makes standing very difficult. Check out the chart below for a variety of g-forces.

Astronauts in orbit	0g
Standing on earth at equator (standard)	1g
Skateboarder on first descent from vertical to horizontal	2.5g
Human sneeze	3g
Street luger rounding a curve	3g
Space shuttle, during launch and re-rentry	3g
Human cough	3.5g
High-g roller coasters	3.6-6.3g
Formula one car, under heavy braking	5g
Ice luge, maximum	5.2g
Apollo 16 rocket, upon re-entry	7.19g
A slap in the face	100g

David is a two-time world champion street-luge racer. Since the equipment and instructions are simple, street luge is easy to learn. But like the Olympic sport of ice luge, street-luge racing requires years of practice. And whereas ice lugers use official tracks, street lugers share the roads with cars, which can be very dangerous.

Wipeout!

Street lugers stick to lonely roads and make sure people called "spotters" watch for traffic.

But accidents still happen. In 2006 David was speeding around a corner, when an SUV ran through an intersection and crashed into him. His luge flew into the air and flipped over. David bounced off and landed on his head, underneath the truck. His helmet split in half. David suffered broken ribs, a dislocated shoulder, and major injuries to his chin and jaw. But he was lucky. Some street lugers have died in accidents. David was out luging again the next week.

Street lugers are closer to the ground than skateboarders, which means they have a shorter distance to fall in a crash!

BMX champion Dave "Miracle Boy" Mirra

In 1993, at the age of 19, U.S. **freestyle** BMX champion Dave Mirra was hit by a drunk driver as he crossed a street. He suffered a dislocated shoulder, fractured skull, and blood clots on the brain. Doctors told him that the trauma to his head would prevent him from ever riding his bike again.

But six months later, Dave was back on his bike. Since then, he has racked up 24 medals at the Summer X Games, the most of any athlete ever. He has also undergone at least that many injuries from the sport itself, including a ruptured spleen and punctured liver. But these injuries never slow him down for long.

WHAT IS BMX?

BMX stands for "bicycle motocross." The sport involves racing or jumping a special, heavy-duty bicycle over an obstacle course.

DID YOU KNOW?

Dave Mirra was the first rider ever to land a double backflip in competition. He also landed the first-ever no-handed 360 backflip.

Extreme roller: Aaron Fotheringham

Aaron Fotheringham may use a wheelchair, but that does not mean he just sits around. You will find Aaron, a Las Vegas teenager, at the skate park with skateboarders and BMX bikers, practicing the same moves as the other athletes. Aaron, who lost the use of his legs at age three from a birth defect called spina bifida, practices a sport he calls "hardcore sitting." It has also been called "wheelchair skateboarding."

SURVIVAL SCIENCE

"No matter what the future brings, I will never give up."
—Aaron Fotheringham

Wheelchair flips

Aaron's moves are inspired by BMX and skateboarding, but performing them in a wheelchair can be tougher. When skateboarders launch into the air for a flip, they can control how fast they spin. Skateboarders can go slower by keeping their bodies straight or faster by scrunching their bodies into a ball. So, if skateboarders go into a flip without enough speed, they can tuck in to speed up and complete a rotation. But Aaron cannot tuck his body in any more than it already is. That means he must launch into his flip at just the right height to complete his rotation before hitting the ground.

Aaron Fotheringham's sponsor, Colours In Motion, created a special wheelchair just for Aaron, with four-wheel shock absorption to help cushion his landings. This makes it easier for Aaron to perform the same sorts of tricks as skateboarders and BMXers.

In 2006 Aaron became the first person to successfully complete a backflip in a wheelchair, a stunt that landed him in Guinness World Records. He practiced the flip about 50 to 60 times into a foam pit. Then, he tried another 15 times on a ramp, which resulted in some spectacular crashes, usually on his head. He was even knocked unconscious a few times. "My helmet has saved my life more times than I can count!" says Aaron.

Extreme running: Danelle Ballengee

Danelle Ballengee is an **adventure racer**. In adventure racing, athletes run long-distance races that consist of a combination of sports, such as paddling, hiking, running, and mountain biking. Danelle had accomplished hundreds of awe-inspiring feats, including climbing all 54 of Colorado's 4,250-meter (14,000-foot) peaks in 15 days.

But in December 2006, she lay crumpled on the floor of a canyon in Moab, Utah, unable to walk or crawl. Night was falling quickly, and so were the temperatures. Danelle was wearing only a thin fleece jacket. Her dog and running partner, Taz, circled around her.

That morning, Danelle had driven to the canyon for a quick, 16-kilometer (10-mile) winter training run. But as she climbed up a rocky part of the path, she slipped on a patch of invisible black ice and tumbled 18 meters (60 feet) downward. She landed on her feet, but the impact broke her pelvis. She collapsed onto her back. Danelle knew she needed to move to a more visible area if she was going to be found. She began to crawl, but only one leg worked. It took five hours for her to creep almost half a kilometer (a quarter mile).

Onward!

Three days after her fall, a police detective found Danelle's van in the canyon parking lot. A 12-person search and rescue team spread out over the 10,120-hectare (25,000-acre) park. Soon a rescue party was greeted by Taz, and he guided them right to his owner.

Danelle spent three months in a wheelchair with a plate in her pelvis. But less than five months after her ordeal, Danelle participated in a 96-kilometer (60-mile) Adventure XStream Race that included mountain biking, running, and kayaking. As the only female in an all-male race, she finished fifth out of fourteen.

SURVIVAL SCIENCE

How did Danelle keep herself alive?

By the time Danelle reached the hospital, she had lost a lot of blood from internal injuries. Doctors said that most people with her injuries would not have lived more than 24 hours. How did Danelle survive for three days in the cold canyon? She put her training to work!

In the canyon, Danelle spent hours doing sit-ups to keep her body warm. She also wiggled her fingers inside her clothes and tapped her toes, to delay **frostbite**. She wore a shower cap, something many extreme runners carry, to prevent the loss of body heat through her head. She had two raspberry gel packs—an energy food—with her to eat. And she sipped small capfuls of water from a nearby puddle. Then there was Taz, who kept her warm at night and led searchers to her side.

Adventure racer Danelle Ballengee's extreme training and conditioning helped save her life after a dangerous fall.

HIT THE SLOPES: EXTREME SKIING AND SNOWBOARDING

It is May 26, 1970, and world champion speed skier Yuichiro Miura is about to do the impossible: ski down the tallest mountain in the world! Starting at Mount Everest's highest southern peak, almost 8,000 meters (26,000 feet) above sea level, the Japanese skier will race 2,440 meters (8,000 feet) down the icy mountain. But at the bottom of the slope is the world's largest bergschrund, a kind of deep opening. Yuichiro must stop short of this giant gap, or he will plunge to his death.

Yuichiro wears a helmet with a built-in two-way radio. Strapped to his back is a parachute, to help slow his descent. Attached to his body is an **oxygen** tank. On his feet are skis. A rescue crew is scattered up and down the mountain.

Yuichiro says a prayer. Then he pushes off. His skis hit the gray, glazed ice. Yuichiro soars downward at 171 kilometers (106 miles) per hour. His parachute opens late. Then, instead of slowing him down, it starts dragging him down. Yuichiro tries to brake, but the ice is too hard. His left ski hits a rock and snaps off like a toothpick. Now Yuichiro is sliding on his spine. He sails over a tree, which launches him 10 meters (33 feet) in the air. He lands on a small patch of snow. Then, miraculously, he stops—just 76 meters (250 feet) from the bergschrund! Yuichiro plants his ski poles in the ground and tells himself not to move.

Yuichiro plans to scale Everest again in 2013. He will be 80 years old. But this time, he will walk down!

Japanese skier Yuichiro Miura was the first person to ski at an **altitude** higher than 8,000 meters (26,000 feet). He has said he was "99 percent sure" he would not survive the experience.

SURVIVAL SCIENCE

How did Yuichiro prepare?

Skiing down Everest is not something you can practice! But Yuichiro spent years planning his expedition. And he traveled with a large crew that included scientists and doctors. After the unit reached base camp, at 5,354 meters (17,600 feet), Yuichiro spent several weeks getting used to the oxygen levels, which are 50 percent lower than those at sea level. This allowed his lungs to gradually expand and absorb more oxygen. He also practiced skiing with a parachute in the thin air.

THE MAN
WHO SKI
DOWN
VERES

Aerial skiing: Speedy Peterson

Jeret "Speedy" Peterson stood at the opening block. It was the 2010 Vancouver Olympics, in Canada, and the U.S. skier was preparing for his second jump in the men's **freestyle aerial** skiing competition. Aerial skiers hurl themselves off a high, snow-covered ramp at 72 kilometers (45 miles) per hour. They then twist their bodies like a pretzel into a series of midair spins and flips, before touching their skis down and landing on the snow below.

At the 2006 Olympics, Speedy had attempted "the hurricane," a move he invented, but he failed to land it. Now, he had a second chance. But could he do it? The hurricane is considered one of the hardest things a person can do on skis. It had never been performed successfully in competition.

Speedy was in fifth place. To win a medal, he knew he would have to do something to give himself an extra edge. He leaped off the ramp and flew 17 meters (55 feet) into the air. He flipped head over heels once, twice, three times, while spinning his body like a top five times around—all in just over three seconds. On his final flip, Speedy spotted the snow-covered ground below. He planted his skis and threw his arms up in joy. He had won a silver medal. Better yet, Speedy had done something no human being had ever done—and survived!

EXTREME TRAINING

Speedy's jumps look impossible—even suicidal! How does he survive? The answer is: years of practice. Here's a peek into training camp for aerial skiers:

In the pool: Before aerial skiers ever hit the slopes, they practice in a pool. The water provides a softer landing cushion.

On the slopes: Landing on the snow from 18 meters (60 feet) in the air is hard on their bodies, so aerialists must limit their practice jumps to about 20 a day.

On the trampoline: On a trampoline, skiers can take up to 100 jumps a day. This is a good place to refine their movements.

In the gym: Aerial skiers must fight against **g-forces** as they move from vertical to a 70-degree angle at 64 kilometers (40 miles) per hour. They lift weights so they can be strong enough to keep their bodies straight when faced with that pressure. Landing (or falling) from so high in the air is rough on the body. Lifting weights also helps their bodies build the strength they need to withstand these hits.

whatever I'm doing, I'm
ing to walk away saying I've tried
hardest, and I can't ever walk away
ying 'what if.'"—Jeret "Speedy" Peterson

Extreme snowboarding: Tina Basich

In May 1999, world champion U.S. snowboarder Tina Basich was doing a magazine photo shoot of her 720 flip. The day was getting late, and Tina was tired from the shoot. As she launched into the air, Tina realized that she did not have enough speed. She spun around as tightly as possible, but she had not even finished her spin when she realized she was not going to make the landing. She crashed down on the top ledge of the ramp. Her body hit so hard, it actually bounced. The fall landed her in the hospital with one leg bone broken and another with a spiral fracture up one side.

A year after her accident, U.S. snowboarder Tina Basich placed second at the Sims Invitational World Snowboard Championships in "Big Air" snowboarding.

Back on board

It was a year before Tina could compete again in the World Championships. With only a few days of practice on a much smaller ramp, Tina was nervous. Should she attempt another 720? She felt she needed to prove to herself she could do it. She had pictured the motions in her head many times while she was recovering. Sure enough, her body remembered. The landing was not perfect, but Tina didn't care. "I was so incredibly relieved and happy," she said.

What went wrong?

Tina blames her fall on her mental state that day. It was nearly summer, and her mind was on warm air and flip-flops—not snowboarding. Even after recovering from her injury, Tina still feels pain in her ankle every time she snowboards. "It's a constant reminder to stay in tune with myself," she says.

Snowboarding is a relatively young sport, and an even younger Olympic sport. It was developed by surfers and skateboarders, starting in the 1960s. Men's and women's snowboarding events debuted in the Nagano Olympics in Japan in 1998.

Stomping it: Shaun White

After his first run at the 2010 Olympics men's **half-pipe** event, U.S. snowboarder Shaun White's score was four points higher than his closest competitor. Shaun would take home a gold medal no matter what he did on his second run. The redheaded athlete could simply skate up and down the middle of the ramp. But that is not what Shaun came to Vancouver to do. He came to put down the move he had been practicing on his private half-pipe for almost two years: the double McTwist 1,260.

HOW DID THE MCTWIST GET ITS NAME?

It sounds like something you would order at a fast-food restaurant or a soft-serve ice cream stand. How did the inverted 540 aerial spin known as the "McTwist" get its name? It was named for the "Mc" who invented it: U.S. skateboarder Mike McGill. Mike first landed the trick at a summer skateboard camp in 1984, two years before Shaun White was born.

In 2003, Shaun White became the first athlete ever to win medals in both the Summer and Winter **X Games**, for skateboarding and snowboarding.

At the end of his second run, Shaun launched himself up the 6.7-meter (22-foot) half-pipe wall and 5 meters (17 feet) into the air. Then, he flipped head over heels twice, while jerking his body into three and a half twists. To use Shaun's own words, he "stomped it." His second score beat his own first score.

Dangerous moves

Shaun made it look easy, but the double McTwist is daring, difficult, and dangerous. Other pro snowboarders have been seriously injured trying to land less demanding moves. Just two months before the Olympics, U.S. snowboarder Kevin Pearce crashed while practicing the double cork, a similar trick. Kevin suffered a traumatic brain injury and is re-learning how to walk.

Shaun admits that he was "scared" practicing the move. He chipped a bone in his ankle while testing it on a foam pad. And at the 2010 Winter X Games, just a month before the Olympics, Shaun had bashed his face into the top of the half-pipe during his practice run. His head snapped back and his helmet flew off. He suffered a gash on his chin and a sprained finger. As he waited to go again, Shaun was forced to watch endless replays of the crash on the big screen. But 45 minutes later, he dropped a flawless McTwist 1,260, to win X Games gold.

A SKATER, TOO

Shaun White is more famous for snowboarding, but he is also a professional skateboarder. At the age of nine, Shaun met Tony Hawk at a local skate park. The legend helped train him, until Shaun became a pro skateboarder at age 17.

Shaun proudly displays his Gold Medal, won at the 2010 Vancouver Olympics in the snowboard half-pipe.

Back country: Big fun, big dangers

Injuries are not the only dangers skiers and snowboarders face. If they leave the half-pipes and well-worn paths at ski resorts and hit the "back country"—far-off slopes where few have skied—they risk falling off cliffs, getting lost, or getting buried in snow!

Saved by his cell phone!

In 2007 British snowboarder Thomas Murphy got lost after straying from the main slopes in a French Alps resort. Then, a large mass of snow called an **avalanche** struck, sweeping Thomas halfway down the mountain. Thomas could not climb back up the steep slope. And to go down, he had to jump off several steep cliffs. His last leap knocked him **unconscious**.

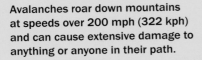

Avalanches roar down mountains at speeds over 200 mph (322 kph) and can cause extensive damage to anything or anyone in their path.

Thomas woke up hours later, in pitch darkness, to find himself trapped on a narrow, icy ridge, over 1,524 meters (5,000 feet) in the air. He reset his cell phone—and got a signal! He called the French rescue services. He also called his family to send his love, because he did not think he would make it out alive. But soon he heard a helicopter. He waved his phone in the air. The pilot spotted the light from over three-quarters of a kilometer (half a mile) away and used it to pinpoint Thomas's location.

Lost!

When U.S. hockey player Eric Le Marque went for a quick snowboarding run at California's Mammoth Mountain in 2004, he left his cell phone behind. After "shredding" down some fresh powder slopes, he realized he was lost. After five days, his family learned that Eric was missing and alerted the police.

Two days later, a helicopter spotted Eric sprawled out in the snow. He had kept himself alive for a week by eating pine nuts and drinking river water. He built igloos to sleep in. But he had lost almost 14 kilograms (30 pounds), and his feet were so painful from **frostbite** he could only crawl. He was taken to a hospital, where both of his feet were **amputated**. Today, Eric snowboards and plays hockey— using **prosthetic** legs.

Your lifeline!

A cell phone could save your life. If you are in trouble, you should:

> Call "911" in North America. Even if you cannot get a signal from your own network, other nearby networks are required to connect you to an emergency center.

> If you cannot reach any network, keep your phone on. It should still show up as a "blip" on your network's screen and help rescuers track you to within 25 to 100 meters (82 to 328 feet).

> Try texting. Text messages transmit in more places than calls.

EXTREME CLIMBING: MOUNTAINEERING AND FREE-SOLO ROCK CLIMBING

On May 26, 2008, headlines around the world announced the sad news: "Australian Mountaineer Lincoln Hall Dies on Mount Everest." Lincoln was a well-known outdoor-enthusiast who had over 30 years of climbing experience. But Lincoln's story was not over yet.

Lincoln had made it to the top of Mount Everest. His trouble began on the way down. In an area of Everest called "the death zone," he developed a form of **altitude** (height) sickness called cerebral edema. His brain swelled, which caused him to start to **hallucinate**, or imagine things that were not real. Then he collapsed. His **sherpas** (guides) tried to carry Lincoln down, but in his confused state he fought them. They did not make it far before Lincoln collapsed again. This time, Lincoln did not respond to their attempts to revive him. Concluding Lincoln was dead, the sherpas left him in order to save their own lives. They reported his death when they made it home.

The next day, U.S. climber Dan Mazur and his team spotted Lincoln on the edge of a cliff, about 8,500 meters (28,000 feet) up. He was half-naked but still breathing. Dan shared his **oxygen** supply with Lincoln and poured him hot tea. He also called a rescue team—who sent sherpas and a stretcher. Lincoln was still hallucinating and suffering from **frostbite**, but he improved as he moved down the mountain. Lincoln lost the tips of his fingers and one toe to frostbite, but otherwise he made a full recovery.

"How could you get a good sleep at night thinking that you passed somebody who needed your help? I mean, that's just the way I was raised."—U.S. climber Dan Mazur

SURVIVAL SCIENCE

Back from the dead

When the sherpas left Lincoln, they were certain he was dead. Lincoln did not even respond when they poked his eyes. How did Lincoln's condition improve after being left overnight in the cold? In addition to altitude sickness, Lincoln likely suffered from severe exhaustion. After sleeping through parts of the night, it is possible that his body was in a better position to heal.

Guides help climber Lincoln Hall down Mount Everest a day after he was left for dead near the top.

Free-solo rock climbing

It is 2007 and U.S. athlete Steph Davis rubs chalk on her hands, tightens her shoes, and begins her ascent. She is climbing the 300-meter (1,000-foot) vertical, granite rock face of Diamond Pervertical Sanctuary in Colorado. She has no rope or safety equipment—just her body and the rock.

As she climbs, the air gets thinner and chillier. Loose rocks tumble down the wall as she struggles to find footholds in the tiny crevices. There is nothing to block the view below, but Steph does not look down. Fear would distract her. As her arms reach for the wall above, her fingers hook into small cracks. From below, Steph looks like a tiny ant crawling up a 100-story building. At the top, Steph sits quietly, watching the birds fly by.

World-record climber Steph Davis practices the sport of **free-soloing**, an extreme form of rock climbing—and one of the most dangerous. Free-solo climbers climb rock faces without ropes, safety equipment, or climbing gear. Falls are usually fatal.

When she's not climbing, free-soloist Steph Davis is preparing her body for climbing. She hikes 16 kilometers (10 miles) up mountains twice a week, practices on her homemade climbing wall, hikes through knee-deep snow, runs trails, and balances on a slackline (loose tightrope) hung high in her yard.

Why does she do it?

Steph describes free soloing as "pure freedom," since she can do it completely on her own, without any equipment. She also enjoys becoming part of the natural world. She believes that risk triggers thought, and she uses the quiet time hanging off the side of rocks or sitting at the top to figure out things in her life. She sees free-soloing as "an expression of mastery," something that many years of rock climbing has prepared her to do.

NEW METHODS: DEAN POTTER

U.S. athlete Dean Potter, who was married to Steph Davis, is himself one of the world's best climbers. He also practices **BASE jumping** (see page 46). Before he free-solos, Dean straps an ultralight parachute to his back. That way, if he cannot make it up the wall he is climbing, he can glide down. He calls this "free BASEing." He is the only person who does it, because of the extreme dangers. The parachute does not have a lot of time to open before Dean reaches the ground, and the parachute

Dean Potter hopes to turn a fall into flight, by strapping a parachute to his back when free-soloing.

could end up crashing him into the wall he is jumping from. Before climbing, Dean rigs a **baseline** (loose tightrope) that spans from the wall he is climbing to the other side of the canyon. So, if he cannot climb higher, or if bad weather or the shape of the wall prevent him from jumping, he will climb *down* the rock until he reaches the baseline. Then he walks to the center of the line and jumps from there!

UP IN THE AIR: WIRE WALKING, SKYDIVING, AND BASE JUMPING

It is August 7, 1974, and Frenchman Philippe Petit wipes the sweat off his palms and reaches for his balancing pole. A wire, less than 2.5 centimeters (1 inch) thick, connects the north and south towers of the World Trade Center in New York City. He is almost half a kilometer (a quarter mile) above the streets of New York City. As the morning sun lights the buildings, Philippe steps onto the wire. Seagulls and airplanes fly just overhead. A feeling of freedom replaces Philippe's fear.

Down below, crowds crane their necks to see the tiny figure floating in the space between the two towers. Traffic stops. The police see him, too. They gather on the tower rooftops and shout at Philippe to get down. They tell him he is breaking the law. But when Philippe reaches one tower, he flips on his heels and heads back toward the other. He dances, then balances on his back. After almost an hour, he salutes, glides to the edge, and surrenders to handcuffs. His sentence: to perform a high-wire act for the children of New York. Philippe is delighted!

SURVIVAL SCIENCE

Balance

Philippe's extreme high-wire act seems impossible, even insane. For anyone without training in wire walking, it would be. But Philippe had practiced every day since he was a teenager.

In his World Trade Center stunt, Philippe's biggest danger would have been to accidentally cause the wire to rotate as he walked, since **gravity** would pull him around with the wire. To avoid this, Philippe had to keep his center of gravity (the place in his body where his weight is concentrated) directly above the wire. His balancing pole helped, because it delayed the force of gravity from acting on him. This gave him time to re-center his body without falling. Also, the drooping edges of the pole lowered his center of gravity, helping him balance.

Philippe Petit and a group of his friends got the wire from one World Trade Center tower to the other by attaching one end to an arrow and shooting it with a bow!

"If you see how carefully I prepare for any kind of walk, legal or illegal, small or big, you will see that actually I narrow the unknown to virtually nothing. And that's when I am ready to walk on the wire." —Philippe Petit

Extreme skydiving: Adrian Nicholas

On March 12, 1999, the airplane glides 10,927 meters (35,850 feet) above the English countryside. British skydiver Adrian Nicholas is ready to jump. Most skydivers jump from only 4,900 meters (16,000 feet). But Adrian has a goal: to break the world record for the longest unassisted flight, meaning the longest flight without using a parachute or engine. The door opens, and Adrian plunges headfirst toward Earth. He will "fly" in his wingsuit for as long as possible, before finally opening a parachute to land (see the box).

It is a windy day, and the pilot and ground crew almost immediately lose contact with Adrian. After 30 minutes, no one can find him. Finally, a ground crew spots him walking. A strong crosswind has blown him sideways. But Adrian has broken the world record! He flew for over four minutes before opening his parachute, landing over 14 kilometers (9 miles) from where he exited the airplane. Adrian has "flown" farther than any human being ever has.

Dolly Shepherd: Parachute queen

In 1904, British parachutist Dolly Shepherd was hired by a London circus to jump out of hot-air balloons. One day, Dolly was scheduled to jump with another female parachutist, then glide, side-by-side, to Earth. After jumping, the other woman's parachute failed to open, so Dolly quickly instructed the woman to grab onto her. The woman clutched Dolly. Unfortunately, the weight of both women was too much for Dolly's parachute. They landed hard, and the impact **paralyzed** Dolly. But after a few weeks of electric shock treatments, Dolly's paralysis disappeared. Within only a couple of months, she was parachuting again.

SURVIVAL SCIENCE

Birth of the wingsuit

Over the years, many people have tried to invent wings for humans. Almost as many have died testing them. Finally, in 1998, Adrian Nicholas helped develop a "wingsuit" that worked. The suit is a one-piece jumpsuit with webbed fabric between the legs and under the arms. At high **altitudes**, air inflates the fabric to create semi-rigid "wings," which lift the body. People wearing the wingsuit soar through the air like flying squirrels, and they descend more slowly than skydivers in **free fall**. But they still need a parachute to slow themselves before hitting the ground.

Adrian rented an air tunnel to test the wingsuit. He also practiced jumping from airplanes at greater and greater heights, to get used to the thin air at high altitudes. High altitude jumping is risky because of the change in air pressure. This can cause confusion or even paralysis. So, before heading up for a jump, Adrian would "pre-breathe" pure **oxygen** for an hour. This helped Adrian avoid "apoxia" (oxygen starvation) in the thin air.

Wingsuits slow a skydiver's free fall, allowing the skydiver to glide more slowly through the air.

World's best BASE-jumping team: Heather Swan and Glenn Singleman

Heather Swan and her husband, Glenn Singleman, have just spent 22 days climbing Mount Meru in Tanzania, East Africa. Then, at 6,604 meters (21,667 feet), they put on wingsuits. The Australian couple hold hands, run to the edge, and throw themselves off the cliff! They free fall for over two minutes, then open their parachutes and glide to a glacier below. It is 2006, and Heather and Glenn have just shattered the previous record for the highest-ever **BASE jump**.

"Once you know the real risks and prepare yourself against them, then you know the real reward. In our case, it was being able to fly off one of the most beautiful mountains in the world." —Glenn Singleman

To prepare for the jump off Mt. Meru, Heather and Glenn practiced 150 skydives together, 60 with wingsuits. They trekked to the base of the mountain in 2005, took pictures, and studied wind patterns.

What is BASE jumping?

BASE jumpers leap from fixed (non-moving) objects, rather than airplanes. "BASE" stands for some of those objects: Buildings, Antenna, Spans (bridges), and Earth (a cliff or other natural structure).

BASE jumpers typically jump from heights lower than skydivers, which would seem to make the sport safer. But BASE jumping is actually far more dangerous. Skydivers jump from about 4,900 meters (16,000 feet). This gives them 45 seconds to open a parachute. Most BASE jumps are much lower, leaving the jumpers only a few seconds to open their chutes. Also, skydivers have nothing but sky around them as they fall. But BASE jumpers risk hitting the side of the object from which they jump.

Over the edge

By 2006 Brazilian-born-U.S. skateboarder Bob Burnquist had already crushed the competition with four gold medals at the **X Games**. Bob's latest passion was BASE jumping. He decided to combine his skills with one incredibly dangerous stunt. The setting: the Grand Canyon. His plan:

to skateboard off a 12-meter (40-foot) ramp, "grind" (slide) onto a thin, 12-meter (40-foot) rail, then roll off the rail into the huge opening below. He would open his parachute before he hit the canyon floor.

On his first attempt, Bob missed the rail and spiraled out of control. His crew of friends, family, and sponsors lost sight of him after he toppled off the ramp, close to the canyon wall. But Bob managed to steady himself and open his parachute just in time. After making some adjustments to the rail, he tried again. This time, Bob successfully skateboarded and BASE jumped his way into the record books. After landing, he heard the sound of cheers and applause throughout the canyon, echoing his awesome feat.

Skateboarder and BASE jumper Bob Burnquist landed on his feet after plunging into the Grand Canyon on a skateboard.

A streamlined pressure suit like this one would protect humans from the extreme heat they would generate by hurtling back into Earth's atmosphere from outer space.

Space diving: The next frontier?!

Picture this: You are aboard a rocket, almost 100 kilometers (60 miles) above Earth's surface. That is 10 times higher than planes fly. You see stars glimmering in the blackened sky above, and Earth is far, far below. You pat your space suit and double-check your parachute straps. The door swings open—and you somersault into space. You soar at 4,025 kilometers (2,500 miles) per hour—faster than any human has traveled without a vehicle—while Earth's horizon rushes at you. After seven minutes of free fall, you open your parachute and float to the ground.

Sound like an awesome dream? Or a horrific nightmare? Either way, this could become a reality. Two space experts have formed a company called Orbital Outfitters. Their goal is to create a special space suit that will allow humans to safely jump to Earth from outer space. "We want this to become the world's most extreme sport," says one owner. For thrill-seekers, space diving could become the ultimate dive. But the special suit could also help astronauts return safely to Earth if something went wrong on a mission.

On a mission: Felix Baumgartner

But who would be "crazy" enough to test such a suit in space? Enter Felix Baumgartner, an Australian skydiver and BASE jumper. Felix has "flown" over the English Channel wearing a "carbon wing," a set of 1.8-meter (6-foot) wings. He has also jumped off the world's tallest building. Felix and a team of experts are planning a jump from 37 kilometers (23 miles) above Earth. If successful, Felix would break the existing record for the longest and highest free fall. After this, a space jump is a mere 60 kilometers (37 miles) away.

What next?

In another 25 years, space diving might not even seem that crazy. It might be as common as surfing—or skydiving. By then, humans will still be exploring new possibilities, things that we cannot even imagine today. As long as there are humans, we will continue to push our limits and reach for the next extreme adventure.

MORE EXTREME SPORTS SURVIVAL FACTS

Would you rather kayak than curl up with a book? Do you prefer bungee jumping to basketball? If so, like many of the people discussed in this book, you may have a "thrill-seeking" gene.

About 15 percent of people have an extra-long version of a gene called D4DR. (Genes are units in the body that determine our different traits, or characteristics.) These people may have a harder time producing **dopamine**, a brain chemical that triggers feelings of pleasure. So, they sometimes seek out thrilling activities as a way to produce more of this pleasure chemical. Brain studies also show that thrill-seekers may experience a bigger emotional bang from exciting activities than others. For thrill-seekers, extreme sports can be a great alternative to more dangerous activities, like smoking, drugs, or criminal behavior. Extreme sports can be risky, but they produce a healthier "high."

PRESSING IT

Are you bored by household chores? Well, perhaps the "sport" of extreme ironing is for you! When Englishman Phil Shaw came home from work one sunny day in 1996, he had piles of laundry to press. But he really wanted be outside rock climbing. So, he compromised. He attached an extension cord to his iron and brought it outside with his ironing board. When Phil's roommate saw him pressing shirts in their backyard, he asked Phil what he was doing. Phil said the first thing that came to mind: "Extreme Ironing."

It started as a joke, but soon Phil and his friends ran with the idea. They ironed while rock climbing, climbing trees, and skiing in the Alps (one person wore a board on his back and the other ironed, as they raced down slopes). From there, the idea only picked up "steam." Now, the sport has a following of about 1,500 people from all over the world. They have pressed shirts underwater, in canoes, while parachuting, and in the middle of city streets. Fortunately, extreme ironing has a good survival rate. The most dangerous part? Burning yourself with the iron. What's next? Extreme vacuuming?

IDITAROD TRAIL INVITATIONAL: SURVIVAL OF THE FITTEST

Alaska's Iditarod Trail Invitational calls itself the "longest, most remote winter ultrarace in the world." Most Iditarod races involve sled dogs, but here no dogs are allowed. Humans must power themselves, using skis, a bicycle, or their own two feet! The finish line is 1,770 kilometers (1,100 miles) away, and the average temperature is –23°C (–10°F). Food is dropped to contestants at two points along the journey. Most competitors carry a tent, sleeping bag, and extra food— on their backs.

Only highly skilled athletes can sign up, and 90 percent of them never finish. In 9 years, only 28 men and 2 women have completed the race. Peter Basinger is one of them. In 2007 he won the race on bicycle in 18 days, 4 hours, and 33 minutes. That was slightly faster than the winner of the Iditarod dogsled race, which was held later that year. Says Peter, "You're alone out there. You redefine your outer limits."

GLOSSARY

adventure racing long-distance race consisting of a combination of sports, such as mountaineering, paddling, hiking, running, and mountain biking

aerial up in the air

altitude height above sea level

amputate cut off a body part, usually by surgery

anaerobic exercise that increases strength but does not require the use of much oxygen

avalanche large mass of snow, ice, or rocks from a mountain slope, sliding suddenly downward

BASE jumping parachute jump from the tops of tall, non-moving objects, usually from about 300 meters (1,000 feet) or less

baseline wire, similar to a tightrope, strung between two points high in the air

bergschrund deep crack or crevice at the upper end of a mountain glacier

concussion injury to the brain, caused by a violent blow or harsh impact

condition train something, such as the body, to get used to doing something

dopamine group of chemicals in the brain that help regulate movement and emotion

free diving sport of diving as deep as possible into the water without oxygen

free fall when gravity is the only force acting on a body as it falls through space. This also describes the part of a parachute jump before the opening of the parachute.

free-soloing extreme form of rock climbing without ropes, safety equipment, or climbing gear

freestyle kind of sport without set rules that is open to new tricks and ideas

frostbite injury or destruction of skin and underlying tissue that results from continued exposure to freezing temperatures. It most often affects the nose, ears, fingers, or toes.

g-force short for "gravitational force," a pressure that acts on the body as it speeds up or changes direction

gene units of cells in the body that determine traits, or characteristics

gravity force exerted by large bodies such as Earth. Gravity holds us onto the surface of Earth.

half-pipe U-shaped ramp used by snowboarders and skateboarders to provide a takeoff for a jump

hallucinate experience imaginary visions or sounds as if they are real

kinetic energy energy of motion

oxygen gas that occurs in Earth's atmosphere and water. Nearly all living things need oxygen to breathe.

paralysis inability to move. Paralysis can be temporary or permanent.

prosthesis device that substitutes for a missing part of the body

sherpa mountain guide. Sherpas often live in the mountains where they help others.

street luge sport of sliding down a sloping street in a specially made sled (called a "luge"), usually with wheels

tourniquet tight band used to control bleeding

tow-in surfing extreme kind of surfing in which surfers hold onto a rope attached to a Jet Ski to get close to the biggest waves

unconscious without awareness, sensation, or mental ability

vital organ organ in the body that is essential for life, such as the heart, kidneys, and liver

X Games sporting competition in which athletes compete in extreme sports

FIND OUT MORE

BOOKS

Bailer, Darice, and Jack Dickason. *Dive: Your Guide to Snorkeling, Scuba, Night-Diving, Free Diving, Exploring Shipwrecks, Caves, and More!* (*Extreme Sports* series). Washington, DC: National Geographic, 2002.

Basich, Tina. *Pretty Good for a Girl: The Autobiography of a Snowboarding Pioneer*. New York, NY: HarperCollins, 2003.

Callery, Sean. *Defying Gravity: Surviving Extreme Sports* (*Extreme Science* series). Mankato, MN: Capstone, 2008.

Figorito, Marcus. *Friction and Gravity: Snowboarding Science*. New York, NY: PowerKids, 2009.

Hamilton, Bethany. *Soul Surfer: A True Story of Faith, Family, and Fighting to Get Back on the Board*. New York, NY: Pocket, 2004.

Hawk, Tony. *Tony Hawk: Professional Skateboarder*. New York, NY: Regan, 2002.

Roberts, Jeremy. *Skydiving! Take the Leap* (*The Extreme Sports Collection* series). New York, NY: Rosen, 1999.

DVDS

Extreme. Washington, DC: National Geographic Video, 2008.
Watch world champion athletes as they ski and snowboard untouched
mountain peaks, climb vertical, frozen waterfalls, and surf some of the
world's largest waves.

Man on Wire. Los Angeles, CA: Magnolia, 2008.
This tells the true story of high-wire walker Philippe Petit's death-defying walk
between the World Trade Center towers in 1974.

The Man Who Skied Down Everest. Chatsworth, CA: Image Entertainment,
2005.
This movie recounts the true story of world champion skier Yuichiro Miura's
climb up Everest—and his descent, on skis.

Popular Mechanics for Kids: X-treme Sports & Other Action Adventures. Port
Washington, NY: Koch Vision, 2005.
Learn how to survive street luging, extreme snowboarding, wind-driven water
skiing, and other extreme sports from experts, including Olympic athletes.

WEBSITES

http://espn.go.com/action/
Learn more about different many extreme sports at this website, which
includes X Games coverage and blogs written by extreme athletes.

www.tonyhawk.com
Visit Tony Hawk's official website and view photos, videos, and more.

www.shaunwhite.com
Visit Shaun White's website for more about him, and to see videos of some
of his most amazing moves.

INDEX